Dear Cassandra & Jo'
To Two wonderful
people — may God continue
to bless you both
Love
Rose Marie
7-1-99

Thoughts That Stem From The Rose

Thoughts That Stem From The Rose

by

Rose Marie Lowe

*I am the rose of Sharon,
and the lily of the valleys.
Solomon 2:1*

RayRose Publishers
Blackwood, New Jersey

RayRose Publishers
P.O. Box 532
Blackwood, NJ 08012

©1992, 1999 Rose Marie Lowe.
Grandmom Miller, © 1978, 1999 Rita Frio, used at her own request.
ALL RIGHTS RESERVED. Published 1999.

"What We Weave in Life", previously published in the following compilation and newspaper: Sullivan, Caroline ed., *Wind in the Night Sky.* (Owings Mills, Maryland: The National Library of Poetry, 1993), page 458; Van Cleef, Robin ed., "Blackwood Poet Published," *United Methodist Relay.* 1993, 38 (July-August, No. 6): page 13.

"Our Future Belongs to the Children," previously published in this compilation: Purcell, John J. III, ed., *Outstanding Poets of 1994.* (Owings Mills, Maryland: The National Library of Poetry, 1994), page 343.

Printed on permanent/durable acid-free paper and bound in the United States of America.

No part of this book may be reproduced in any form, by electronic or mechanical means, except by a reviewer who may quote verses in a review, without permission in writing from the publisher.

Library of Congress Card Number 98-92135

ISBN 0-9666862-0-9

Design Credits:
      Typography, Carolyn Cordelia Williams, AHLP Communications, an imprint of Africana Homestead Legacy Publishers, Cherry Hill, New Jersey.
      Cover Design, Brian Lancaster, Omega Group Concepts, III, Inc., Philadelphia, Pennsylvania.
      Photography, Livingstone Harvey, Willingboro, New Jersey.

I dedicate this book of poetry, first, to my Lord and Savior Jesus Christ whom I love very much and who gave me these words of inspiration. These teaching and uplifting poems are not mine, but His. I am His vessel and I am truly thankful that He loves me so much that He uses me to tell of His Love, Faith and Hope. To Him I give honor and glory. He is worthy to be praised.

I also dedicate this book to my husband Raymond, whom I love also very much. Raymond is always by my side, always helping, always there when I need him. He is not only my husband, but my friend and my inspiration.

Thoughts That Stem From The Rose

Contents

I am the rose of Sharon, and the lily of the valleys. Solomon 2:1.

About the Author	x
Acknowledgments	xi
Preface	xii

Part I   Love

Greet one another with a holy kiss. 2 Corinthians 13:12.

The Little Book on the Shelf	2
Life Is God's Most Precious Gift	5
Give from Your Heart	8
Learn to Love One Another	10
Life Is Fragile, Handle It With Prayer	13
Let Us Forgive	15
Re-Introduced to My Lord	17
Two United as One	20
Love	22
Two Hearts Joined as One	23
He Stepped Aside	25
God Bless the Woman	27
Thank God for Mother's Day	29
Let the Little Ones Come Unto Me	31
Sharing God's Love	32
I Have a Friend Named Jesus	34
How Hard Is It to Say I Love You	35
Woman	36
Grandmom Miller (Rita Frio, author)	39

Part II   Faith

We Live by faith not by sight. 2 Corinthians 5:7.

What We Weave in Life	42
Our Future Belongs to the Children	44

Come and Follow Me	46
You May Stumble Many Times on Your Way	48
Invite Jesus to Come In	50
Have You Touched the Hem of His Garment	51
Stop and Take Time to Pray	53
He Is Not Dead, He Is Alive	55
He Lives Forever More	56
Death Is Like Going Through Another Door	58
He's Coming Back	59
Faith - The Victory	60

Part III   Hope

Then I heard the voice of the Lord saying, Whom shall I send? And who will go for us? And I said, here am I, send me. Isaiah 6:8.

Tears of Repentance	62
The Wages of Sin Is Death	64
Reflection in the Mirror	66
Let Our Light Shine Together	68
The Key to Unlock the Door	70
Behind Closed Doors	72
A Message of Hope	74
Happy Thanksgiving Day	76
The Holy Child	78
"Forgive Them Father for They Know Not What They Do"	80
Out With the Old, In With the New	82
Our Promise Is Jesus	84
Thank You Jesus	85
The Blessing of a Vision	87

About The Author

The second of three daughters of Clifford A. Simpson (deceased) and Laura M. (nee Jones) Simpson. I was born March 7, 1942 at Cooper Hospital in Camden, New Jersey. My sisters are Elnora Cain and Edith, "Edie" Simpson. Receiving my education in public school, I graduated from Triton High School in Runnemede, New Jersey. While working at R.C.A. in Camden, New Jersey, I met Raymond Lowe. We fell in love and were married. Raymond and I have two beautiful daughters, Crystal Cooper and Tina Turenne, who gave us six wonderful grandchildren–five grandsons–Phillip, Travis, Serge, Warren and William (twins) and a granddaughter, Jasmine Marie. After attending computer school, I took a position in Maple Shade, New Jersey as a computer operator (keypunch and telekey), entering data for computerized payrolls.

When I was a teenager, I wrote horror stories for Halloween parties causing fright and fun, however, my serious interest in writing emerged later. From childhood I was a very active member of the United Methodist Church. As a born-again Christian, I started writing poetry and had a poem printed in the *Relay*, a newspaper of the United Methodist Church. Two of my other poems were included in collections of The National Library of Poetry: "What We Weave in Life", in *Wind in the Night Sky*, 1993, and "Our Future Belongs to the Children," in *Outstanding Poets of 1994*. I attended Camden County College for public speaking. I became a certified lay speaker, speaking in my own church and also visiting other churches.

I was nominated by and presented a plaque by the late Mayor Ann Mullen of Gloucester Township, for "A woman that makes a difference in Gloucester Township." I have been a Gloucester Township Committee woman since 1994, and I am dedicated to helping improve my community.

I pastor as a temporary fill-in minister at a church in Lindenwold, New Jersey.

My dream was to write a book of religious poems and have them published one day. My dream has come true through the grace of God with His blessings.

Acknowledgments

Thank you,

to my daughters, Crystal Cooper and Tina Turenne , for their love, understanding, and unbiased criticism;

to my mother, Laura Simpson, who always supported me with her steadfast belief in my poetry;

to my sisters, Elnora Cain and Edith "Edie" Simpson, who assisted me and continue to help me in every way;

to my former pastor, Tom Beauford, and his wife Beverly, who not only inspired me to write poetry but gave me that extra little push, opening a new and exciting door to my life with Jesus Christ;

to my cousin, Carolyn Cordelia Williams, for making my dream come true.

Thoughts That Stem From The Rose

Preface

    This collection of poems was written to uplift those who may be heavy hearted, those who have lost hope and need to renew their faith, or just to make hearts glad. On many occasions, I would awaken in the wee hours of the morning and listen to the words of the Lord pouring out from my mind and heart. Sometimes my pen would have a hard time keeping up with the spiritual thoughts in my mind.

    I was blessed with this poetry that teaches and inspires all to love and hope!

    During my involvement in prison ministry, Jesus also rewarded me with a special group of inspirational poems for the men at the Riverfront Prison in Camden, New Jersey: *Behind Closed Doors; The Key to Unlock the Door; A Message of Hope*. These religious verses were especially meant to sustain the inmates and give them hope during their incarceration.

    The words to *The Little Book on the Shelf* were given to me so quickly, I had trouble organizing my thoughts. Although the poem was in my mind, at first, I did not know the right beginning. Then, I was awakened at 3:00 A.M. and was blessed with the opening verse.

    Let Our Light Shine Together is about a little old church on a hill, a historic site that still opens its doors for all. *Re-Introduced to My Lord* is the testimony of my life, of how I changed, yet came back to God and gave him my life.

    My former minister, Pastor Tom Beauford, would prepare his sermons, then call me, sometimes the night before service, to ask me to write a poem that would coincide with his message. "If the Lord blesses me with one," I would say. My pastor never doubted and he was continually right. I always had new stanzas to read just before his sermon.

    These poems are from my heart through the blessings of God. I hope at least one, if not all, will touch your heart so that you may be uplifted in the Lord.

                             God bless you all.

Part I

Love

Greet one another with a holy kiss. 2 Corinthians 13:12.

THE LITTLE BOOK ON THE SHELF

I looked upon a shelf
In a bookcase on the wall
It was put up long ago
When I was very small

In the corner on a shelf
Was a book that looked brand new
It seemed to be pushed aside
Or just hidden out of view

A layer of dust it had on it
The name you could barely see
As I blew off some of the dust, I saw
An H-O-L-Y and a B-I-B-L-E

I couldn't believe my eyes
This surely could not be
This precious book called the Bible
Tucked away where no one could see

There were many books on the shelves
That were written and filled with sin
It seemed those dedicated to Satan
Had their covers and pages worn thin

Thoughts That Stem From The Rose

Well, I reached out my hand, and touched this Holy book
And removed it from off of the shelf
I continued to dust off the cover,
While I said a short prayer to myself

I tenderly, lovingly, opened this book
Its pages so crisp and so new
A joy began to take over
Filling me through and through

I started reading this little book
And began to re-unite with my friends
From Adam and Eve to Malachi
To Jesus on into the end

Yes, I read from the Old Testament, and on into the New—
What a wonderful re-union that was
I started humming and singing, because
I was filled with spiritual love

There was so much love in this book
And many miracles too
But most of all I found faith
For it's there to carry you through

Thoughts That Stem From The Rose

Without faith, what would we have
Or just where would we be
Faith is being sure of what we hope for
And certain of what we don't see

Whoever owned this precious book
And wanted it to hide
Has missed so many wonderful things
That are written down inside

Now it's cover is crinkled and wrinkled and worn
Yes, I keep it right next to my bed
And its pages are thin and some of them torn
For this book is most constantly read

Oh, it lights up my life
When I think to myself
Thank you dear Jesus—for letting me find
This little book on the shelf

LIFE IS GOD'S MOST PRECIOUS GIFT

Life is God's most precious gift
We must keep it wrapped in love
For it was given to us
From our Heavenly Father above

He blesses some with long lives
Some may have their time cut short
But whatever the will of God
He is there to strengthen and support

Perhaps we're not as agile as we would like
Or our health not as good as it used to be
Perhaps our minds aren't quite as alert
And our eyes aren't as sharp to see

Our footsteps might not be as fast
And our strength has gone a bit
We sometimes have to stop for breath
And find someplace to sit

Perhaps there is no bread
Upon your table for you to eat
Or perhaps at your table
There remains an empty seat

Thoughts That Stem From The Rose

From a friend or a relative
Who is no longer here
Just the memory of one
Of whom you hold so dear

Perhaps you feel you've lost your friends
Or you have no job anymore
Perhaps you are so lonely and sad
You feel everyone has closed their door

Well, whatever cross you're bearing
Have no fear in any way
Because Jesus is still carrying you
Each and every day

Don't worry about tomorrow
Or dwell on yesterday
Just live your life for Jesus
And just live it day to day

If we're not as agile as we used to be
And our health is not in fit
If our footsteps have slowed up
And we tire just a bit

Thoughts That Stem From The Rose

If there's no bread upon the table
Or we have an empty chair
Trust in Jesus to console us
For His love is everywhere

When you feel so all alone
And it seems that no one cares
All your friends have not forsaken you
Because Jesus is still there

God gives us strength to carry on
Our life from day to day
In whatever we do, wherever we go
And in whatever we say

If you have problems in your life
Just accept our Lord above
For life is God's most precious gift
And we must keep it wrapped in love

GIVE FROM YOUR HEART

There are people who are rich
There are people who are poor
And there are people who are stingy
That are always wanting more

These people just won't help
No matter what you say
They continue to be selfish
Day after day

Well, What if God was selfish
And stingy with His love
What if He kept us
From Heaven above

What of our salvation
We surely would be lost
We'd better loosen up our hearts
No matter what the cost

Let's open up our hearts
And open up our minds
To walk the road of Jesus
And to treat others kind

Thoughts That Stem From The Rose

And when we're doing these things
Let's all remember to give
Not just our smiling face
But in the way we live

Let's help one another
And don't forget your church
For tithes and offerings unto God
Is a blessing of true worth

Now let's remember the widow
Who put in two copper coins
This lady gave all her money
That she needed to live on

While yet the rich did give their gifts
It was certainly just a part
God gave the widow a special blessing
For giving from her heart

We all are asked to do the same
And now is the time to start
Whether it's a gift of money or love
Make it a gift from your heart

Thoughts That Stem From The Rose

LEARN TO LOVE ONE ANOTHER

Be careful how you live your life
In all the things you do
Because the way you live it
In the end will tell on you

Be thoughtful and be kind
To everyone you know
Help others whenever you can
No matter where you go

There are people who are hungry
Some are homeless on the street
Give your love like Jesus would
To these people that you meet

Help them in any way
Whether its money, food or love
Give with a caring attitude
Like our Heavenly Father above

We must be careful in what we do
And also in what we say
For we may have to relive it
In another passing day

Thoughts That Stem From The Rose

We are whom God has created
Woman and man
He has joined us both together
And keeps us hand in hand

So let us get together
And share Gods glorious love
Learn to love one another
As our God loves us above

For love is born of faith
Believing Jesus is God's only son
Who died on the cross, then rose again
To offer salvation to everyone

Love is patient and kind
We must treat others good
Love one another
In the right way that we should

Love is not jealous or boastful
Meek and humble we should be
All glory must be given to God
In whatever we do or see

Thoughts That Stem From The Rose

Love is not irritable or resentful
Neither is it arrogant or rude
It does not insist on having its way
And is never proud, loud or crude

Love does not rejoice at wrongs
But it rejoices in the right
We must rejoice like the Angels in Heaven
Everyday and every night

Love bears all things, believes all things
Love shall never fail
It hopes all things, endures all things
Yes, God shall prevail

Let your light shine out of darkness
With faith, hope and love
Walk in the ways of Jesus Christ
Our dear sweet Saviour above

LIFE IS FRAGILE, HANDLE IT WITH PRAYER

We are tempted every waking day
For Satan is everywhere
And the only way to handle it
Is to do it with prayer

Remember, Jesus was tempted with Satan
After those forty nights and forty days
Well, Satan is still out here tempting
Only in different ways

As the tempter told Jesus
Make bread from these stones
Jesus replied
Man does not live on bread alone

We must continue trying
To do the best we can
To give up things we tempt for
Again and again

We must learn how to sacrifice
To do as Jesus said
For other things in life
Are more important than just bread

Thoughts That Stem From The Rose

Life is just so fragile
And Satan's waiting to come in
To fill your heart of lust and greed
A heart that's filled with sin

We must be careful in what we do
And also in what we say
For we may have to relive it
In another passing day

So when we're in the days of Lent
And we're sacrificing too
Remember God who sacrificed
His only son for you

Make any sacrifice you want
And do it with the best of care
For remember life is fragile
Handle it with prayer

LET US FORGIVE

We must stand on one accord
In the way that we live
We must love one another
And be willing to forgive

For divided we fall
Together we must stand
Always put God first
Let Him keep us hand in hand

Don't talk bad about one another
Don't repeat what others say
Stop being overly sensitive
And take time out to pray

Stop holding grudges
Don't be complaining all the time
Give your burdens up to Jesus
And start treating others kind

If we wish to be FORGIVEN
We must learn to be FORGIVING
So ask Jesus to teach us
To change the way we're living

Thoughts That Stem From The Rose

Let go of your childish ways
And in God put your trust
Forgive your trespassers
As God forgives us

Ask our Father in Heaven
Our dear sweet Saviour above
To remove all jealousy and anger
And to replace it with love

Live in harmony with one another
Do not take revenge
Don't repay evil for evil
It's up to God to avenge

Be joyful in hope
Keep sharing God's love
Be compassionate to one another
As our God is from above

Let us unite together
In the way that we live
To love one another
And always to forgive

RE-INTRODUCED TO MY LORD

I've known my Lord Jesus
Since I was a little girl
I was taught He gave His life
To save this sinful world

But as I grew up
And became a little older
Sin came in strong
And my heart became colder

Satan seemed to have found a place
And there he wanted to stay
Temptations, greed, jealousy and anger
Always seemed to come my way

God was always there
But He seemed to be in a fog
My heart was given to Satan
And no longer belonged to God

Thoughts That Stem From The Rose

Never letting me feel good
This sin seemed to take God's place
All it ever left me with
Was an empty, empty space

Well, I've been re-introduced
To my Saviour up above
There's no longer greed, anger or jealousy
I now feel only love

So when you feel real empty
And nothing seems to go right
Get on your knees and pray to God
Whether its day or night

Pray to Our Saviour and pray with faith
And mean what you say to Him
For if it's His will—it will be done
And you'll always win

Thoughts That Stem From The Rose

You just can't lose when your trust in God
He's always there for you
Don't push Him aside and know Him not
For you He will always be true

I now have committed myself to Jesus
And I will say to you
I will go with Him where He wants me to go
And do what He wants me to do

So, If there's nothing in your life
And you're always feeling bored
Do as I did, and do it now
Get re-introduced to my Lord

Thoughts That Stem From The Rose

TWO UNITED AS ONE

Marriage is the union
Of two people in love
And it comes from the blessings
Of our Heavenly Father above

May there be long years
That you will stand together
And the sharing and caring
In all kinds of weather

The bitter and sweet, pleasure and pain
In order for dreams to come true
It takes sacrifice and sometimes tears
Shared only from the both of you

Sometimes love is neglected
And many times it's abused
Ignored, misguided, untrusted
Sometimes love is misused

Be attentive and truthful
Compassionate and wise
Use tenderness, gentleness
And keep God first in your lives

Thoughts That Stem From The Rose

Blessed are the two
Who will walk in love
More blessed are the two
Who walks with God above

Be submissive to one another
Be gentle and kind
Listen and understand
With the heart, not the mind

Love one another for love is God
And as you walk with Him each day
Respect each others privacy
But kneel together when you pray

May this bond in Holy Matrimony
Bring much happiness and peace
Enjoy your married blessings
Day by day they will increase

The best of everything to you both
As your new life has just begun
May God Bless you and keep you —Always
    TWO UNITED AS ONE

LOVE

Love is born of faith
Believing Jesus is God's only Son
Who died on the cross, then rose again
Offering salvation to everyone

Love is patient and kind
We must treat others good
Love one another
In the right way that we should

Love is not irritable or resentful
Neither is it arrogant or rude
It does not insist on having its way
And never proud, loud or crude

Love does not rejoice at wrongs
But rejoices in the right
We must rejoice like the Angels in Heaven
Every day and every night

Love bears all things, believes all things
Yes, God shall prevail
It hopes all things, endures all things
Love shall never fail

Let your light shine out of darkness
With faith, hope and love
Walk in the ways of Jesus Christ
Our dear sweet Saviour above

Thoughts That Stem From The Rose

TWO HEARTS JOINED AS ONE

Two lonely people—two lonely hearts
Both—
Living a life of emptiness
Both living not too far apart

She didn't really understand
Why she was always feeling sad
He didn't understand as well
Why he felt so very bad

They just lived their life in motion
In a world that had no love
They weren't aware of Jesus
Or our Heavenly Father above

A friend invited her one day
To come visit at her church
She really didn't feel up to it
But she thought what could it hurt

And so it seems another friend
That lived not far away
Decided to pay a visit
To that same church that day

This friend invited him to come
And go along to church
He really didn't feel up to it
But he thought what could it hurt

Thoughts That Stem From The Rose

So these two lonely people
And their friends who were so glad
Traveled to church together
The two of them still feeling sad

But somewhere in the message
As the minister continued to preach
The glory of the Lord came down
And touched their hearts so deep

Their eyes lit up and their minds as well
No more dark and dreary days
The emptiness was gone away
God changed their thoughts and ways

For they accepted Jesus Christ
Our Savior Lord that day
And He made them clean and pure
In a most holy and Christ-like way

As they looked into each others eyes
It was certain that they knew
Their lives had changed in a different way
A feeling of love so true

Two lonely people, two lonely hearts,—No—
Their new lives have just begun
For in finding Jesus, they found themselves
Two hearts are now joined as one

HE STEPPED ASIDE

Sometimes through life
Our dignity and pride
Will make us a little selfish
And keep us from stepping aside

We must all have a chance
To do the things we should
Obey our Father in Heaven
The way that Jesus would

Answer to His call
Whatever it may be
To teach others the best you can
And to change the wrongs that you see

Some may talk about guidance and truth
Some on understanding and love
They may tell of patience and kindness
That comes from our Father above

We thank and praise God
That no dignity and pride
Has kept some pastors
From stepping aside

Thoughts That Stem From The Rose

They've allowed the lay persons
To do their part
To preach God's message
Straight from the heart

Now, this can only happen
If a door is opened wide
And we're allowed to enter
Because someone's stepped aside

To hold back God's word
No more shall it be
You shall hear the Gospel
From out Father's laity

We are all blessed with gifts
That are sent from above
We must use them or lose them
For God gave them with love

We shall glorify our Saviour
With the love we have inside
And to be joyful and thankful
That the Pastors stepped aside

GOD BLESS THE WOMAN

We thank God for taking
A rib from Adam's side
And for creating woman
For man's dignity and man's pride

A woman must be gentle
In things she'll often do
But, she also must be strong
For the trials that she goes through

A loving hand, understanding heart
A tender touch
The shedding of tears
And forgiving much

It took a woman called Mary
Who lived here upon the earth
To bring forth a son
That she named Jesus at birth

For Mary, it took acceptance and faith
To believe in our God above
We women need this also
And, we need another called love

Thoughts That Stem From The Rose

For whenever we're feeling weary
With so many troubles on our mind
We can give them all to Jesus
Who is so gentle and so kind

We are woman that God has created
A companion He put with man
He's joined us both together
And keeps us hand in hand

God watches over the woman
Because He's so sweet and so good
He helps us to do the right things
And to obey Him the way that we should

Oh, We love you dear Heavenly Father
For saving us all from sin
Whether we're male or female
Your open arms welcome us in

THANK GOD FOR MOTHER'S DAY

There is a day that's set aside
That we call Mother's Day
It comes just once a year
On Sunday and in May

We're told that we are special
And we are treated oh so well
These children of ours love us
Or so to hear them tell

But wouldn't it be nice
If this was every day
That all this attention
Was headed in our way

Because you see my children
We love you everyday
We sacrifice for you
Not just in the month of May

Not just one day of every year
That is specially set aside
But every minute God gives us breath
Our love for you abides

Thoughts That Stem From The Rose

So let us get together
And share God's glorious love
Let us love one another
As our God loves us above

Let's do it every day
Of every single year
He'll fill our hearts with gladness
With joy and lots of cheer

And every day will be Mother's Day
Not just once a year
God strengthens our love, perfects our life
So when we shed a tear

A tear of joy or sorrow
We will be able to say
Thank you God for allowing
Every day to be Mother's Day

LET THE LITTLE ONES COME UNTO ME

Let the little children come unto me
This is what Jesus said
Handle them gently—fill them with love
Keep them spiritually fed

And when a child has grown
And his church attendance is lack
He will still have Jesus in his heart
So he surely will be back

Let's keep our children coming out
Every Sabbath Day
We'll continue to teach everyone of them
How to kneel and how to pray

Don't let Satan steal their hearts
And Sinners they end up to be—
For remember what Jesus said
Let the little ones come unto me

SHARING GOD'S LOVE

We are blessed with many things
For this we are grateful to God
But we must remember to share His love
And not keep it hidden inside

Bring others the news of Jesus
How He died on the cross for our sins
Open your arms and open your heart
And welcome others in

We must all share His love
And we're asked to do our part
So let your love spread from within you
And enter into other hearts

Let us not be selfish with God's love
For if we truly care
We will fill other hearts and other minds
So that they in time can share

Thoughts That Stem From The Rose

The glorious joy from Jesus
Knowing that He is alive
Believing in Him and trusting—For
He's the only way to survive

When you share your love, your abundance won't lessen
It will only get bigger each day
Let the light shine brighter in your heart
So that you may show others the way

Read your Bibles daily
And pray to our Father above
Always ask Him to help you
And remember to share God's love

I HAVE A FRIEND NAMED JESUS

I have a friend named Jesus
He's with me wherever I go
No matter the time—Whether day or night
Jesus is there I know

He promises to never leave me
By my side He'll always be
I can depend on Him all the time
Because He truly loves me

In the wee hours of the morning
When you dare to call on the phone
Call on our Lord Jesus Christ
In the quietness of your home

Whether you're sick or healthy
Whether you're joyful or sad
Get on your knees and pray to Him
And tell Him both the good and the bad

Tell Him what's on your mind
And tell Him just like it is
He won't condemn you, He'll love you
For depending on His great blessedness

Yes, I have a dear sweet friend
A friend who's so good to us
I'd like those who haven't, to meet Him
My friend whose name is Jesus.

Thoughts That Stem From The Rose

HOW HARD IS IT TO SAY I LOVE YOU

How hard is it to say I love you
To share a good word or two
Let people know exactly how you feel
And what you would like them to do

Open your heart and open your mind
And let all three words come out
Don't hold it in or whisper it
Let it out with a great big shout

I love you, I love you
Say it some more
It's easy to say
It's so good and so pure

So look at each other
And say with a smile
I really love you
And say it a while

Don't hold your feelings back
If you know it to be true
It's so easy to tell it like it is
So say the words, I love you

Thoughts That Stem From The Rose

WOMAN

Thank you God for taking
A rib from Adam's side
And for creating woman
For his dignity and his pride

We are woman that you have created
A companion you put with man
By joining us both together
And keeping us hand in hand

Sometimes we're oh—so weary
With many troubles on our minds
Then we think of you my Jesus
Who is so gentle and so kind

We think of Noah's wife
In the flood that covered the earth
And we think of the virgin Mary
Who gave our Lord Jesus His birth

Thoughts That Stem From The Rose

Of the faith and acceptance it took
To believe in our God above
Not only did they need these two words
But they needed another called love

So look upon us women
Dear Jesus so sweet and so good
Help us to do the right things
And obey you the way that we should

We love you dear Heavenly father
For saving us all from sin
Whether we're male or female
Your open arms welcome us in

SPECIAL DEDICATION

I first met the late Rita Frio (May 26, 1932-January 19, 1999) at Mt. Zion Church in Albion, New Jersey. Pastor Lula Harris is the minister there.

One Sunday Rita recited a poem she had written called *Grandmom Miller*. It touched my heart in such a way I can't describe.

When Rita came up to the front of the church and started speaking, her voice was so soft and gentle, yet soothing and true. We knew this lady loved the Lord with all her heart and that was where she was speaking from (her heart).

She says, "the poem just came in my mind so fast I could hardly write it down on paper." She doesn't know why she was blessed with it, only God knows. I think this was God's plan years ago that it be included in my book of poetry so that it might touch the hearts of many.

My sister and I thought Rita might be an angel put here on earth, however, when we asked she said, "No, honey, I'm not an angel, ask my husband." Her husband John, who is one of the nicest men I have ever met, was so in love with his wife, it seems that's the only reason for life.

God joined these two beautiful people together and blessed them as one.

Rose Marie Lowe, 1999

Thoughts That Stem From The Rose

GRANDMOM MILLER

Grandmom Miller, as we called her, sat with anticipation on her face.
"It must be her, 'best blue dress' you know, the one with all the lace."
She gave me change to buy a ribbon to match the dress she chose,
And she worried if the dress would 'go' with her shoes and hose.

I remembered how she had come
To be in the old folks home,
On a day about ten years ago,
She had come but not alone.

Her family had accompanied her, two daughters and two sons,
And I could sense the tears she hid till the arrangements were all done.
They kissed and hugged and promised her they would write and visit very often.
For this separation causes grief that these words are meant to soften.

The letters were few, the visits were fewer,
And for the past three years there were none.
And I can't count the times I'd heard Grandmom Miller say,
"Who knows they just may come today!"

And when they didn't then she would say,
"Oh sometimes children are that way,
They just get so busy with their work and families,
That it just doesn't leave much time for me."

Thoughts That Stem From The Rose

She never said these words with bitterness or strife
But, I thought how do they forget so soon the mother who gave them life!
I prayed today would be the one on which they all would come,
Today was Grandmom's birthday and she was 81.

And so with love I helped her bathe and dress
And I brushed her snow white hair,
And as I did she told me of her life
And the memories of the years.

I had heard these stories many times before, but I took the time to listen,
For there is nothing more she loves than when she's reminiscing.
Finally all was done and I left her sitting in the sun—
Because on Sundays visiting begins at One.

At Three I checked to see if her family had arrived
But I found her sitting all alone after how she'd planned and strived.
I went off duty at Six P.M. and I thought it such a shame
That after all her hopes and dreams, no one came.

On Monday when I came in at Nine, my friends told me the news.
Grandmom Miller, had just received four beautiful bouquets
With cards of regret that the birthday greetings had come so late,
But, it really didn't matter anymore. Grandmom Miller, died, at Eight.

Rita Frio, 1978

Part II

Faith

We live by faith not by sight. 2 Corinthians 5:7.

WHAT WE WEAVE IN LIFE

Be careful how you live your life
In all the things you do
Because the way you live it
In the end will tell on you

Remember always to be kind
To everyone you know
Help others whenever you can
No matter where you go

There are people who are hungry
Some are homeless on the street
Give your love like Jesus would
To these people that you meet

Thoughts That Stem From The Rose

Help them in any way
Whether its money, food or love
Give with a caring attitude
Like our Heavenly Father above

For all the good things that you do
You're given a Holy thread
To weave a robe in Heaven
Love thy neighbor, Jesus said

Keep a loving heart and a caring mind
Because in time you shall see
What you weave in life
You will wear in eternity

Also published in the following compilation and newspaper: Sullivan, Caroline ed., *Wind in the Night Sky*. (Owings Mills, Maryland: The National Library of Poetry, 1993), page 458; Van Cleef, Robin ed., "Blackwood Poet Published," *United Methodist Relay*. 1993, 38 (July-August, No. 6): page 13.

Thoughts That Stem From The Rose

OUR FUTURE BELONGS TO THE CHILDREN

Tis so sweet to be so young
You hear older people say
If I could only turn back the time
I'd live my life in a different way

Well living young in this world today
Would certainly be a chore
For these are very trying times
Of poverty, hate and more

Such as drugs and alcohol
Selling these things in our schools
Having to belong in a gang or clique
And trying hard not to break their rules

No, this can't be our youths
That we depend upon their living
To change this sinful world
Into a place of loving and giving

What's happened here
Where did we go wrong
What did we do—
Relax a little too long

Thoughts That Stem From The Rose

Did we forget about Jesus
Forget to tell the story
Did we forget to read the Bible
And tell of all its glory

It's not too late to change the world
We still have a little time
We must offer our prayers to Jesus
For forgiveness to all mankind

Send your children to Sunday School
Have them say their prayers each night
Take them to church with you
Teach them how to worship God right

For our future belongs to the children
And they belong to God above
They must learn to be patient and kind
And above all they must learn how to Love

Also published in this compilation: Purcell, John J. III, ed., *Outstanding Poets of 1994*. (Owings Mills, Maryland: The National Library of Poetry, 1994), page 343.

COME AND FOLLOW ME

Jesus said to Simon Peter
As He was walking by the sea
Cast not your nets upon the water
But come and follow me

For there are things that we must do
Cast not your nets again
You will not be catching fish
From now on you will catch men

Men who have become
A prisoner within
Who allowed Satan
To fill their bodies with sin

For we are always tempted
It happens everyday
Worry not about it
Let Christ lead your way

Bolts and Bars and prison gates
He who has ears let him hear
Through glass and steel and guarded doors
Our Saviors light appears

Thoughts That Stem From The Rose

Bars of separation
Loneliness and despair
Curtains of solitude
All taken away with prayer

Just close your eyes and begin to pray
To our Heavenly Father above
Mean exactly what you say to Him
Because He's of kindness and love

God listens to you, so be sure of your words
And with faith you must pray
Not just once in a while
But pray to our Father each day

He stands at the door of your heart and knocks
Won't you invite Him to come in
Let the blood of Jesus Christ
Wash away all your sins

Our Lord and Saviour loves us
And He says to you and me
Cast not your nets upon the water
But come and follow me

Thoughts That Stem From The Rose

YOU MAY STUMBLE MANY TIMES ON YOUR WAY

We all seek to go to Heaven
And for some that's where we're bound
We must stay on the road to righteousness
For that's where our victory is found

When you decide to take this road
Don't expect it to be wide, smooth and straight
For it's a narrow road with stumbling blocks
That leads to that Holy Gate

I must tell you, this road is not easy
And that you may stumble and fall
But if you've given your heart to Jesus
It won't make a difference at all

Because—He's there to protect you
And He will carry your load
Jesus will pick you up and plant your feet
Right back on that righteous road

Thoughts That Stem From The Rose

Satan's always out to get you
In any way that he can
He'll use you and abuse you
Both the woman and the man

So be aware on that righteous road
For it's filled with stumbling stones
Keep your eyes on the light at the end of the road
And you'll never be alone

Keep asking God to help you
For guidance and for strength
To keep your caring abiding within
And to share His love, at any length

We must leave behind our childish things
And continue to grow every day
Trust in Jesus and never give up
For you may stumble many times on your way

INVITE JESUS TO COME IN

Be kind to one another
Let Jesus cleanse your heart
Make Him the ruler of your life
Right now is the time to start

He stands at the door of your heart and knocks
Won't you invite Him to come in
Let the blood of Jesus Christ
Wash away all your sin

God listens and hears your prayers
So speak to Him each day
He promises to fill your hopes and dreams
In every single way

For anyone born within Christ
Becomes a new creature that's free
In your mind and in your heart
You can be what you want to be

Thoughts That Stem From The Rose

HAVE YOU TOUCHED THE HEM OF HIS GARMENT

There was a woman
Who was as sick as she could be
She didn't know what to do
Or who she should go and see

She saw many doctors
They did all they could
They gave her medicine
But it did her no good

She heard that Jesus
Was coming her way
So she went to see Him
On that special day

She gently touched the hem of His robe
And she was instantly healed
Her faith had made her whole again
God's infinite power is real

Because, without faith, what would we have
Or just where would we be
Faith is being sure of what we hope for
And certain of what we don't see

Thoughts That Stem From The Rose

And what of our faith —do we believe
That Jesus can do all
Will we reach out to touch His hem
And answer to His call

Have You reached out your hand
And gently touched His hem
Has He blessed you now
As He blessed others then

It's not too late, just take His hand
And follow in His light
Keep praying to our Saviour
Both day and night

Just love your Lord with all your heart
And do the best you can
For all you really have to do
Is reach out and touch His hem

STOP AND TAKE TIME TO PRAY

Have you ever wondered
Just why we kneel and pray
So many of us do it
Each and every day

We speak to our Divine Majesty
Our Heavenly Father above
Who listens to us always
With patience and with love

He wants to hear our stories
Of things we've done that day
And how we had to struggle
With Satan's sinful way

Of how we try to do the best
In everything we do
We must walk in Jesus's footsteps
For God keeps His hand on you

He shares with us in sorrow
And smiles with us in joy
He watches over the aged
And blesses the little girl and boy

Thoughts That Stem From The Rose

He wants us to ask for His blessing
Of the sick and of the poor
For those on drugs or alcohol
He'll open up the door

He promises to never leave
By your side He'll always be
So keep sending up your prayers
And in time you'll surely see

Your blessings overwhelming
Coming down to you from above
Filled with joy and with laughter
Filled with honesty and love

So remember, no matter how tired
Or how busy you seem to be
Take time out for Jesus
I do —and He's always with me

Whatever you want to do
Whatever you want to say
Whatever you have on your mind—Always—
Stop and take time to pray

HE IS NOT DEAD, HE IS ALIVE

For God so loved the world
He gave His only son
To die upon the cross
To save us, everyone

They nailed Him to the cross
They didn't even care
No water would they give Him
Such pain He had to bear

Jesus died upon the cross
Our sins were such a burden
He died to please His Father
Our God, which art in Heaven

He is not dead, He is alive
Our Jesus, Lord of lords
For He was resurrected
And will live for evermore

HE LIVES FOREVER MORE

It was early in the morning
On the first day of the week
After Jesus was crucified
And things were dim and bleak

That Mary Magdalene, Joanna
And Mary, the mother of James
Were on their way to visit
The tomb where Jesus laid

However, as they neared the tomb
They saw Jesus was not there
Hallelujah, He had risen
And left that tomb completely bare

Only but the strips of linen
And the burial cloth for Jesus head
Were all that were left there
Jesus was not dead

Then, an Angel appeared before them
And he gleamed of glistening white
They quickly bowed before him
For they were terrified with fright

Thoughts That Stem From The Rose

"He is not here, He has risen"
The Angel clearly said
"You must look for the living
Do not look among the dead"

For the Son of man was crucified
And on the third day rose again
He will live forever
His life shall never end

If we take Jesus in our hearts
Our life shall never end
But we must accept Him all the way
And trust Him as our friend

Yes, Jesus was resurrected
It is truly a great joy
All who know our Lord and Saviour
Knows He lives forever more

DEATH IS LIKE GOING THROUGH ANOTHER DOOR

Death is like opening another door
To a world of beauty beyond
Of bright colors and happiness
And a greater peace of mind

There we'll see our precious Jesus
In the brightest of brightest lights
Whose voice will be of the softest voice
And His gown of the purest white

His tone will not be condemning
And His love for us we will feel
We'll want to throw our arms around Him
But at His feet we'll surely kneel

Shedding tears of joy and love
Knowing we're safe with our Christ
Hearing beautiful singing and laughter
Forever, our eternal life

It's just like opening up a door
And going through to the other side
To a much different world, with different things
To a world we'll all abide

So praise God's Holy name
And don't be sad any more
Because death will be exactly
Like going through another door

HE'S COMING BACK

Keep a watchful eye and stay in prayer
For that special day when we meet in the air
Our Savior is coming—what a joyous return
Christians taken into Heaven —sinners left here to burn

In those hot flames of fire and brimstone in Hell
Look in your Bible, Revelations will tell
Of the second coming of our Lord Jesus our King
With Angels beside Him—He promises to bring

He'll separate us—the good from the bad
He'll take up the living as well as the dead
We'll go to His glorious Heaven above
With Jesus and His Angels and oh so much love

The pearly gates will be open and we'll all enter in
We'll be happy in Heaven because there's no sin
And we'll live with our Jesus whose so clean and so pure
Our God will watch over us forever more

FAITH—THE VICTORY

A battering weed, He will not break
A smoldering wick He will not put out
Until justice is put to victory
And our faith has no doubts

That God is our Heavenly Father
Jesus His only son
Who had to die, then rise again
To save each and everyone

Faith is the victory
That overcomes this world
For it defeats old Satan
With his troubles and turmoil

Where oh death is your victory
Where oh death is your sting
We shall live forever
With our Savior, Lord and King

Part III

Hope

Then I heard the voice of the Lord saying, Whom shall I send? And who will go for us? And I said, here am I, send me. Isaiah 6:8.

TEARS OF REPENTANCE

There lived a woman in a city
Who sinned a great sin
But wanted forgiveness
And to become clean within

She followed Jesus to the Pharisee's house
There she began to weep
With the tears from her eye's and using her hair
She washed and dried our Savior's feet

Anointing Jesus with perfume
Humble and kneeling with fright
Repenting within, yet knowing
That He would make everything right

For repentance begins in the heart
Asking God to forgive
Meaning what we say to Him
And changing the way we live

Thoughts That Stem From The Rose

Our God has compassion
This dear sweet Savior above
He pardons our iniquity
And delights in unchanging love

Repentance presents itself in action
Tears of sorrow, thoughts of fear
God does not retain anger forever
With prayer your sins disappear

Pray to our Father in Heaven
For the Kingdom of God is at hand
He will cast your sins into the depth of the sea
From the tears of repentance of man

Thoughts That Stem From The Rose

THE WAGES OF SIN IS DEATH

The problem all started in Eden
A long, long time ago
In a beautiful garden where trees
Of every fruit would grow

In this garden God put Adam
Who was formed from the earthly dust
To rule over the garden
But, in God he was to put his trust

However, Adam was lonely
So from his rib God made Eve
A lovely woman companion
Who in time would disobey and deceive

In the garden was a tree called the Knowledge of good and evil
Of this their choice was not free
For God told them eat of any fruit
But do not eat from this tree

But Eve did eat and Adam did too
They disobeyed God's command
They broke the rule, didn't listen to God
Now, they'll feel the wrath of His hand

Thoughts That Stem From The Rose

Suddenly realizing they were naked
They gathered up fig leaves
Sewed them together for clothing
Then hid ashamed among trees

Satan had deceived Eve
And caused her to fall
Eve deceived her husband Adam
And caused him not to obey God at all

For he ate of the fruit
That he was forbidden to eat
And sinned a great sin
Of deception and deceit

We of today must not be weak like Eve
Or to that crafty shrewd Satan give in
We must always trust and obey God
For death is the only answer to sin

REFLECTION IN THE MIRROR

I looked in the mirror
And what did I see
A reflection of a woman
Looking back at me

I began to think about this world
As I continued to stare
Seeing hardships and struggles
Seeing situations unfair

Sexism, racism, injustice and more
People that are misunderstood
Some that are made to feel second class
And some think that life is no good

But from Jesus comes the gift of hope
From our Jesus, the power of love
Gone is the silent solitary suffering
With blessings from our God above

I saw drugs killing our youths
Alcohol, prostitution and hoods
Doing the evil of Satan
Destroying the things that are good

Thoughts That Stem From The Rose

People facing abuse, rape, and assault
Poverty, oppression, and persecution too
Brokenhearted, facing violence and having no hope
Christ is the only answer for you

Feelings of joy and happiness
Yet accepting the things that we must
God overcomes all things
And its Him in who we must trust

I turned from the mirror
And began to pray
That the blessings from God
Would change things one day

And that the reflection in the mirror
Would show only peace
And the evils of this world
Would finally cease

Then I could look in the mirror
And the reflection I would see
Is a woman who loves God
Smiling back at me

LET OUR LIGHT SHINE TOGETHER

There's a sweet little church
That shines its love on you
And shares its beams of joy
All the whole year through

Standing peaceful and serene
This little church on the hill
Is filled with the Holy Spirit
And is doing God's will

The Lord is still blessing
So come and behold
This sanctuary and surroundings
One hundred forty-one years old

It still opens its doors
They still open their hearts
They welcome you in
To become a small part

Thoughts That Stem From The Rose

Of the light that shines
From this sweet little site
For when small parts gather
They shine a great light

Come and accept Christ
Now is the time to start
To praise and honor Him
Have Him come into your heart

Let your light shine
From the Saviour above
Let our lights shine together
With harmony and love

THE KEY TO UNLOCK THE DOOR

Long ago in Bethlehem
A little child was born
His mother placed Him in a manger
Of hay to keep Him warm

He was Christ our Lord and Savior
Who lives forever more—
Whatever your burdens or sins
He's the key to unlock the door

Many times we feel so weary
Troubles everywhere and everyday
Look up and give them all to Jesus
For He will take your burdens away

You must remember and never forget
To keep Jesus as number one
Make Him always first in your life
And God's will shall always be done

Thoughts That Stem From The Rose

Remember always to be kind
To everyone you know
Help others whenever you can
No matter where you go

In this lifetime you need courage and strength
Because Satan's waiting to come in
To fill your heart with lust and greed
To fill your heart with sin

Always continue trying
To do the best you can
To give up things you tempt for
Again and again

To everyone with unclean hearts
God will bless you even more
If you believe in His son and repent of your sins
He's your key that will unlock the door

BEHIND CLOSED DOORS

Those who stay behind closed doors
Don't be depressed too long
Give your entire self to Jesus
He will uplift you and make you strong

Uplift you in faith and love for Him
Strong in His wisdom and words
Give up your burdens to Jesus
And you'll feel free as the soaring birds

You must believe in God the Father
Who gave His only son
Who had to die, then rise again
To save each and everyone

So, if you're tired and lonely
Maybe you're sad and blue
Perhaps you're somewhat frightened
Of what the future holds for you

Just close your eyes and begin to pray
To our Heavenly Father above
Mean exactly what you say to Him
Because He's of kindness and love

Thoughts That Stem From The Rose

God listens to you, so mean every word
And with faith be sure to pray
Not just once in a while
But pray to our Father each day

Just because these doors are closed
Doesn't mean you can't be free
For in your mind and in your heart
You can be as free as you want to be

You're only a prisoner
In your body with sin
So get rid of Satan
And let Jesus come in

With the love of God—You'll feel free as the birds
And He will bless you with much, much more
Everyone of you can be free
Even though you're behind closed doors

A MESSAGE OF HOPE

Behold, men at Riverfront
God speaks to everyone
God sends to you a message of Hope
To those who believe in His Son

His Son whose name is Jesus
Who gave His life for you
Confess your sins and change your ways
That's all you have to do

Be kind to one another
Let Jesus cleanse your heart
Make Him the ruler of your life
Right now is the time to start

He stands at the door of your heart and knocks
Won't you invite Him to come in
Let the blood of Jesus Christ
Wash away all your sin

Thoughts That Stem From The Rose

Remember, If you're still frightened
Of what the future holds for you
Pray to our Father in Heaven
Let Him make you become brand new

For any man born within Christ
Becomes a new creature that's free
In your mind and in your heart
You can be what you want to be

God listens and hears your prayers
So speak to Him each day
He promises to fill your hopes and dreams
In every single way

To the men who stay at Riverfront
God speaks to everyone
This is the message of hope He sends
To all that believe in His Son

HAPPY THANKSGIVING DAY

How many of us ever stop
To think just what this means
The words Happy Thanksgiving
May not be just what it seems

For when these words are spoken
What comes into your mind
Is it the smell of turkey cooking
Or the pies of every kind

Do you think of all the people
That will gather at your home
Perhaps you will be visiting
Or maybe eating all alone

Well, let's really take a good look
At the world and all it's dreams
Let's analyze it carefully
At just what Thanksgiving means

Let's turn these words around
From Thanksgiving to giving thanks
To God and all His blessings
His understanding and forgiveness

Thoughts That Stem From The Rose

We should thank God for the food we eat
So many tables are bare
Thank God for your health
And for the clothes you wear

But most of all, we should thank God
For sending us His Son
Who died upon the cross
To bring salvation for everyone

Yes be thankful, And be sure to give
The very best you've got
For if you give all of yourself
Then you've given quite a lot

So when you repeat these words again
You'll know exactly what you say
And you will mean every word
When you wish someone "A Happy Thanksgiving Day"

Thoughts That Stem From The Rose

THE HOLY CHILD

Long ago in Bethlehem
A little child was born
Mary placed Him in a manger
Of hay to keep him warm

In a stable He was born
There was no room in the inn
His mother wrapped Him in swaddling cloths
This babe who was born without sin

Oh, what a sweet child He was
As He lay on the manger of hay
Truly He was the Holy child
For He was praised in a special way

There were shepherds in the fields
Watching their flocks by night
When an Angel appeared before them
Surrounded by a glorious light

Fear not said the Angel
For I bring you great joy
In a manger wrapped in cloths
Lays a newborn baby boy

Thoughts That Stem From The Rose

He is Christ the Lord our Saviour
Continued the Angel to say
You will find Him in Bethlehem
In a stable strewn with hay

Then the Angel went into Heaven
And the shepherds went on their way
Hurrying towards the town of Bethlehem
To soon see their Saviour one day

And there they saw our Jesus
So sweet and serene
They praised and glorified Him
His spirit so pure and so clean

Just think, this little babe so small
Who lays upon the hay
Will grow and give His life for us
To save us all one day

Thoughts That Stem From The Rose

"FORGIVE THEM FATHER FOR THEY KNOW NOT WHAT THEY DO"

Oh, the pain our Lord Jesus felt
When they hung Him on the cross
How He must have hurt from the nails they used
When He shed His blood for us.

They took some thorns and made a crown
And placed it on His head
They laughed at Him and mocked Him
And then they crudely said

If you are Christ, then save yourself
Don't let this day be lost
If you are truly the chosen one
Come down from off that cross

But from our precious Jesus
He uttered not a sound
He felt sorry for this sinful world
For He was Heaven bound

They offered Him wine vinegar
To drink upon the cross
And hung Him between two criminals
Whose souls they thought were lost

Thoughts That Stem From The Rose

Our loving Jesus hung His head
And said so plain and true
"Father forgive them
For they know not what they do"

"Father forgive them
For they know not what they do"
Not only did He mean it then
But now for me and you

No matter what we do
Or no matter what we say
Jesus is there to forgive us
Whatever the time of day

You need only just to pray
Forgive me Jesus my friend
And His forgiveness will flow to you
And never —never end

OUT WITH THE OLD, IN WITH THE NEW

God grant us a good new year
As we enter out of the old into the new
Bless us dear Heavenly Father
With love and our faith for you

We thank you for the old year
That you carried us all through
You healed the sick and dying
We're grateful dear Father to you

Many times we were so weary
Troubles everywhere and everyday
But all we had to do was look up to you Lord
And you took all our burdens away

The future belongs to you
We don't know what the New Year will release
So we pray it will bring us your guidance and comfort
As well as good health, joy and peace

Thoughts That Stem From The Rose

We ask you to forgive us from all our sins
That we did in the year of the old
And let us begin a new life
As this new year starts to unfold

And let us remember and never forget
To keep you as number one
You will always be first in my heart
For thine will shall always be done

My heart belongs to you now
And here is where I want you to stay
To always walk beside me
Every single step of the way

My life changed when the old year went out
Now I'm living my life anew
Help others Father to find a new life
Out with the old and in with the new

OUR PROMISE IS JESUS

We've no promise of how long we'll be here
On this earth of sin and lust
We've no promise of how long we'll be here
Just in Jesus we know we must trust

THANK YOU JESUS

I thank you Jesus
For everything you've given me
The air we breathe, the joy we feel
The sun and stars we see

We thank you for our loved ones
You've been so good to me
You've showered me with blessings
That all the world can see

I thank you for my friends
I thank you for my food
I thank you for forgiveness
To me you've been so good

I thank you for dying
On the cross to set me free
Thank you so much Jesus
For just letting me be me

Thoughts That Stem From The Rose

The Blessing of a Vision was written in response to a personal request made by Kay Taylor, the former Gloucester Township historian. Gloucester Township was celebrating its 300th anniversary, and a descriptive poem was needed as a tribute to this rare occasion.

Although I was a long time resident of the area, I needed guidance so that I could write a poem that captured the historical essence of Gloucester Township. Therefore, I prayed and the inspiration for this poem was sent from God.

This poem was presented to Kay Taylor, who in turn facilitated a reading at Mayor Sandra Love's inauguration. After the inauguration, many copies of *The Blessing of a Vision* were printed on parchment paper, placed in the Mayor's office, and made available to the general public.

My involvement with this tribute was a unique experience. Accordingly, I thank God for blessing me with the opportunity and ability to write a poem that represented 300 years of trials, tribulations, and accomplishments of Gloucester Township residents.

THE BLESSING OF A VISION

We give thanks unto God
For He has truly blessed
This place called Gloucester Township
God has given us the best

The early pioneers came
Here they decided to stay
The road was not easy
But, these settlers made a way

For they looked to our Lord
And they knew they weren't alone
Shared each others troubles
As if they were their own

The work was long and hard
The income very low
The outcome great and priceless
Yet little did they know

Thoughts That Stem From The Rose

That from sixteen hundred ninety-five
To nineteen ninety-five
Their pride, endurance and dignity
Would keep this landmark alive

Early industrial activity
Iron products and mills
Farming and cultivating
In both lowlands and hills

Giving hope and dreaming dreams
Of a beautiful new day
Believing and trusting
With God showing the way

Pride of Chews Landing
Is a Senator's former home
St. Johns Rectory and Sickler House
They truly set the tone

Thoughts That Stem From The Rose

There's St. Johns Evangelist Church
Marquadant-Johnsons farm is here
These have such sweet memories
Of treasures held so dear

Chews Methodist Church and Hillman House
They do Glendora proud
The Gabriel Daveis Tavern
And the Ashbrook burying grounds

What about Robert Brewer's home
Determined not to stop
They built the Brewer Homestead too
In this great town called Hilltop

And Blenheim with its beaming joy
A landmark of a home
Stands the Chew-Powell house
That's now most privately owned

Thoughts That Stem From The Rose

In Blackwood stands the Bates Household
A town of sheer delight
With an old school house and post office
A small park that lights the night

Solomon Wesley Church still standing
The First Presbyterian Church too
With the Methodist church of Blackwood
All open and welcoming you

Three hundred years it took
Sacrifice, hardships and sharing
Sweat, tears, life and death
Love, bonding and caring

God has brought us through these years
Neither man nor woman did He skip
In placing a vision within their minds
And giving us Gloucester Township

Thoughts That Stem From The Rose

*...The wilderness and the solitary place
shall be glad for them: and the desert
shall rejoice and blossom as the rose.*

Isaiah 35:1